Peyton Goes to the Dog Show

By Lee Canalizo

Illustrations by Martial Robin

REVODANA PUBLISHING

REVODANA PUBLISHING
81 Lafayette Avenue, Sea Cliff, N.Y. 11579

ISBN: 978-1-943824-00-7

www.revodanapublishing.com

This book is in memory of my friend, Roger Rechler.

A great champion of the dog in general,

and the Afghan Hound in particular!

With faces aglow, we go to the show.

We pay at the gate, and, oh, this looks great!

The first thing we see is a big yellow tent!

And under the tent, we find all the rings.

There are handlers and judges and ribbons and things.

But mostly there are DOGS,

SOOO many to see ...

There are big dogs and small dogs,

short dogs and tall dogs.

There are some dogs that are fluffy,

and lots that look scruffy.

Others are fast and very long legged.

Here is the Azawakh — you never know where he's headed.

Salukis and Greyhounds are so very graceful ...

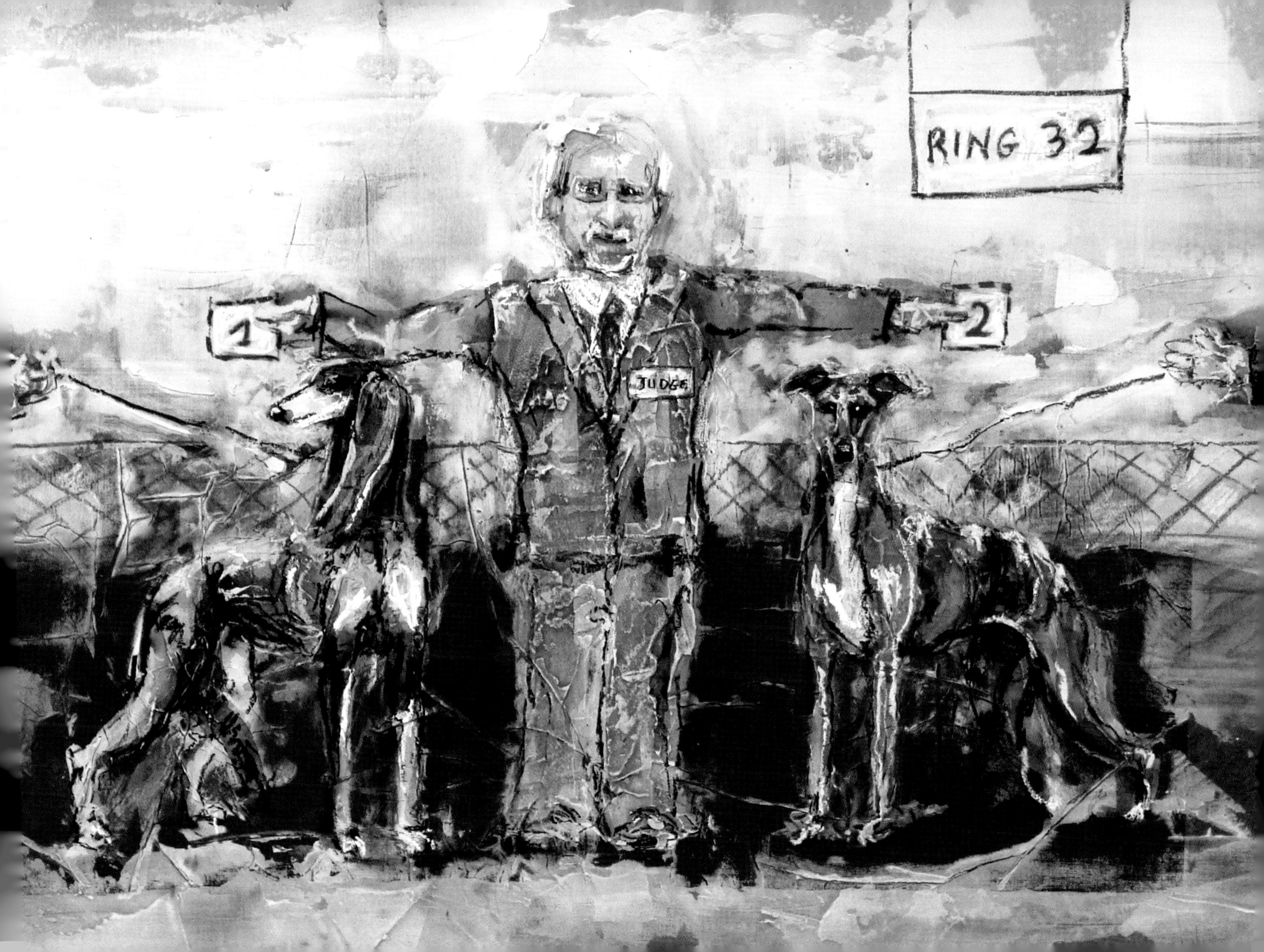
RING 32
1
2
JUDGE

But others have whiskers — a big, furry face full!

The long-legged dogs can run all the day.

The short-legged dogs can't do that ... no way!

Some dogs have red fur,

many come in pure white.

And then there are some that are a beautiful BLUE.

Believe it or not, that really is true!

The Shepherds and Briards work hard herding sheep.

But some do two jobs, like helping police!

Malamutes and Samoyeds plow through snow that is deep.

The Siberian Huskies glide over that slush,

at the command of the driver, who calls out to them, "MUSH!"

The Afghans are glamorous, with

coats silky and long,

While the Komondor is peculiar,

with cords white and strong.

Then there is the Rottweiler, so robust and true.

As opposed to the Chihuahua ...

In one hand, you can hold two!

So many Terriers, both highish and lowish.

There are Airedales and Irish — these are the tallish,

while the Scotties and Norfolk — they are the smallish.

The naughty Bedlington can easily get into a jam.

But he doesn't get scolded, 'cause he looks like a lamb!

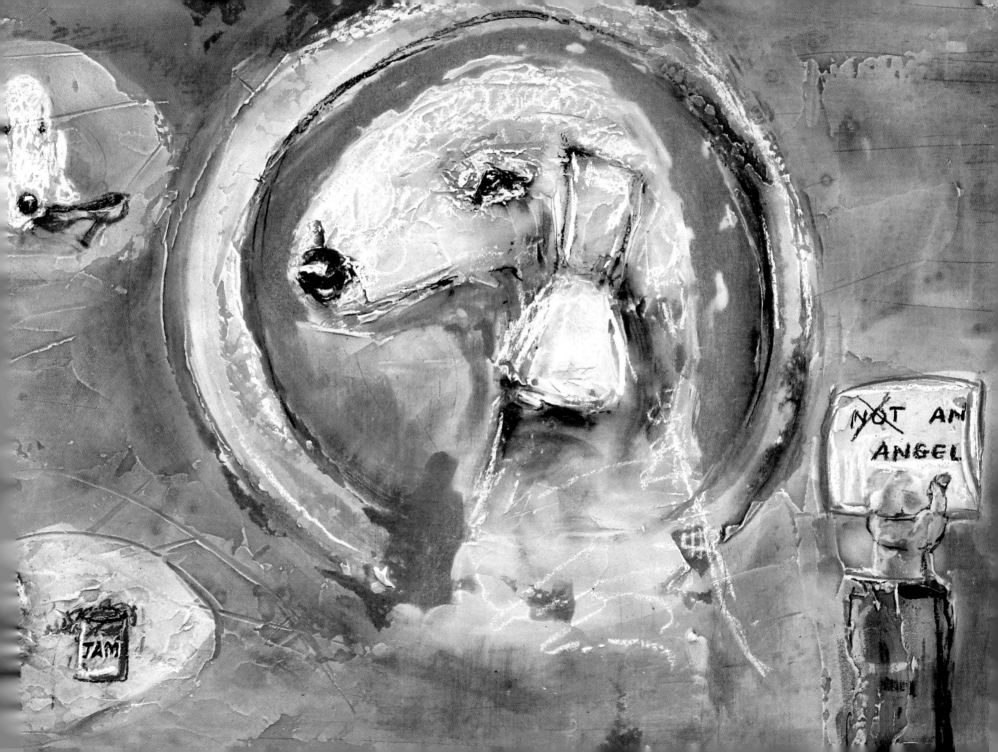

The Spaniels are many — Engies, Cockers and Springers.

With tails merrily wagging, they're friendly humdingers!

The Retrievers and Pointers hunt in their own special way.

They find and then bring home the game of the day!

And say hello to the big fellows, like the Tibetan Mastiff.

With a deep bark and a ruff for his collar,

he'll guard the front gate, and will know when to holler.

Then there's the Neapolitan Mastiff, looking quite scary.

So large, so wrinkled, and not a bit hairy!

And so different, on the other hand,

we have a great little worker, bred in a northern land.

He's a Swedish Vallhund, with a history so deep,

he sailed with the Vikings, but now he herds for his keep.

And soon there will be other breeds joining the show.

More dogs for me and more dogs for you,

doing the doggy things we ask them to do ...

But most of all to be a friend so true!

About the Author

Lee Canalizo of Palm Harbor, Florida, is an internationally known dog-show judge and writer. In a career that has spanned four decades, she has judged at some of the world's most prestigious shows, including the Westminster Kennel Club Dog Show.

This book was born during that very famous show, at the Manhattan townhouse of her dear friend Roger Rechler. Peering out the window at a mounting blizzard, the two soon came to the conclusion that their families wouldn't be able to travel through the white stuff to join them. So they settled in for a spaghetti dinner. As Roger stirred his homemade tomato sauce, Lee started writing this little book of doggy verse. With each sampling and critiquing the other's work, the dinner got made and the book got written.

About the Artist

Martial Robin of Pannecé, France, has always painted animals. Horses have been his favorite inspiration for many years. Then, his passion for dogs and involvement in the dog world inspired him to paint them, too ... especially Afghan Hounds, which have been his faithful companions for many years.

Whether he is painting Poodles or people, Martial sees himself as a portraitist whose work captures more than the flop of an ear or swish of a tail. Reaching beyond a figurative representation of his models, Martial's paintings reveal their inner landscapes as well, becoming a kind of "soul mirror."

Enthusiastically received and highly coveted, Martial's paintings hang in 70 different countries on five continents.

www.peytongoestothedogshow.com